Living Fossils

T0337599

Written by Sally Morgan

Illustrated by Kunal Kundu

Contents

Collins

What is a living fossil?

Dinosaurs

Hundreds of millions of years ago, the earth was covered by vast forests and swamps. It was home to the dinosaurs.

About 65 million years ago, there were huge changes to the world and none of these reptiles survived. They became extinct.

Fossils

Nobody has ever seen
a living dinosaur.
But scientists can work
out what they looked
like from fossils.

Fossils can be formed in
many ways. For example,
when an animal dies,
it may fall into water and
get covered by mud.
Mud falls on top, pushing
down on the layers
below and turning it
into sedimentary rock.
Hard parts of its body,
like the bones, are
preserved inside the rock
as a fossil.

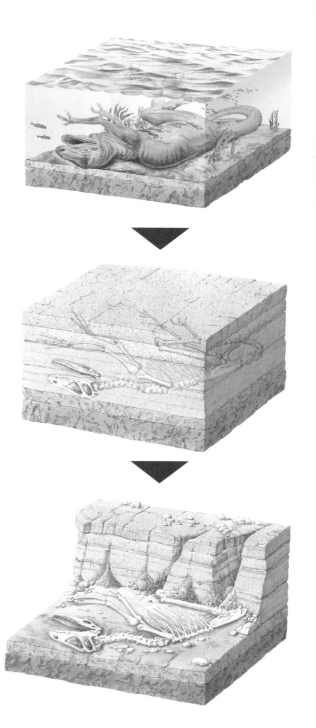

Living fossils

The dinosaurs became extinct, but some plants and animals that lived with them are still around today. We can learn about life on Earth millions of years ago by studying these living fossils.

sea lily or crinoid

nautilus

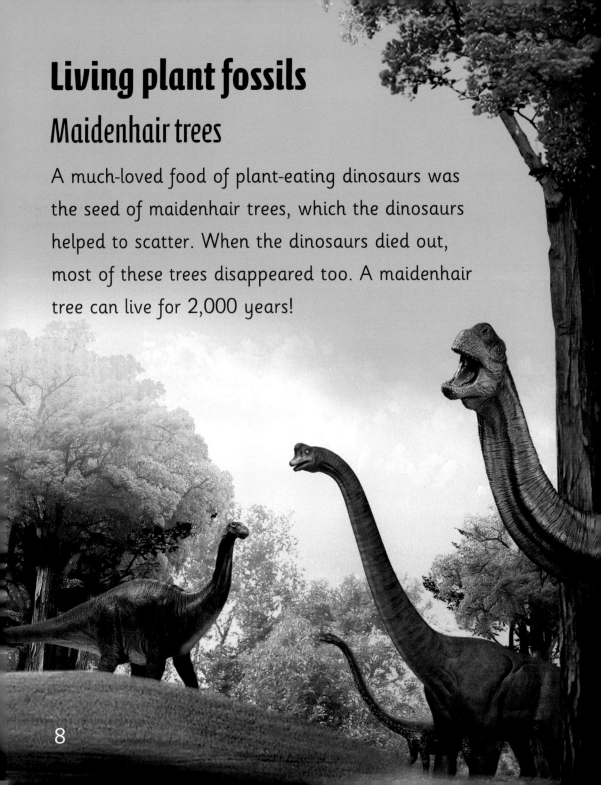

Living plant fossils

Maidenhair trees

A much-loved food of plant-eating dinosaurs was the seed of maidenhair trees, which the dinosaurs helped to scatter. When the dinosaurs died out, most of these trees disappeared too. A maidenhair tree can live for 2,000 years!

Luckily, a few trees of this species survived in Asia.

Today, maidenhair trees are found in parks and gardens.

Found   worldwide

Date back   200 million years

Cycads

Cycads are prehistoric plants that lived in the time of the dinosaurs. A cycad has a trunk, and a crown of stiff leaves at the top.

| **Found** | worldwide |
| **Date back** | 250 million years |

Today, cycads grow in rainforests and deserts, as well as gardens and parks.

Living animal fossils

Horseshoe crabs

In spring, hundreds of thousands of horseshoe crabs gather along the coast of Delaware in America where the females crawl onto the beach to lay their eggs.

These prehistoric creatures are called crabs but they are closely related to arachnids, such as spiders and scorpions.

Found	shallow water off North America, Southeast Asia and East Asia
Date back	500 million years
Food	worms, mussels, clams

Elephant sharks

The unusual elephant shark is named after its
snout that looks like a trunk. They search for
food on the seabed using their snouts.

Found	shallow waters of the South Pacific
Date back	400 million years
Food	shellfish

Tuataras

Tuataras lived at the same time as the dinosaurs.
These lizard-like creatures have four limbs, a spiny crest and
a long tail. Tuataras grow very slowly to about 50 cm in
length and they can live for longer than 100 years.

Found	New Zealand
Date back	200 million years
Food	insects, spiders, eggs

Stinkbirds

Stinkbirds get their name from their smelly droppings. They eat leaves which they digest in their stomach, just like cows. Stinkbirds live in groups and they make a lot of noise that sounds like cows mooing. They do not fly very well and often crash-land. The chicks often fall out of their nest so they use a small claw on their wings to climb back in.

Found	mangrove swamps in South America
Date back	30–35 million years
Food	leaves

Living Fossils

Humans have lived on Earth for 200,000 years, but the animals and plants in this book have been around for many millions of years.

Living fossil timeline

horseshoe crabs

cycads

elephant sharks

500   400   300

millions of years ago

maidenhair tree

stinkbirds

tuataras

200   100   today

After reading

Letters and Sounds: Phases 5–6

Word count: 532

Focus phonemes: /m/ mb /s/ sc c /sh/ si ci

Common exception words: of, to, the, into, are, so, do, were, their, today, water, many, shoe

Curriculum links: Science: Animals

National Curriculum learning objectives: Spoken language: listen and respond appropriately to adults and their peers; Reading/Word reading: apply phonic knowledge and skills as the route to decode words, read accurately by blending sounds in unfamiliar words containing GPCs that have been taught, read common exception words, read words containing taught GPCs and –s, –es, –ing, –ed, –er and –est endings, read other words of more than one syllable that contain taught GPCs; Reading/Comprehension: develop pleasure in reading, motivation to read, vocabulary and understanding by discussing word meanings, linking new meanings to those already known

Developing fluency

- Your child may enjoy hearing you read the book.
- You may wish to take turns to read a page and the fact boxes throughout.

Phonic practice

- Help your child to get quicker at reading multi-syllable words.
- Ask your child to:
  - Read the sounds in each syllable 'chunk' and blend.
  - Then read each chunk to read the whole word.
    di/no/saurs dinosaurs   sci/en/tists scientists
    pre/his/tor/ic prehistoric   mill/i/on million
    scor/pi/on scorpion
- Now read the words quickly without chunking them up.

Extending vocabulary

- Look at page 2 together. Point out the words about types of places, or 'habitats' where animals live or plants grow. (*forests, swamps*)